OUTDOOR LIFE

essential

HIKING

for teens

Kristine Hooks

Children's Press
A Division of Grolier Publishing
New York / London / Hong Kong / Sydney
Danbury, Connecticut

*To Steve Holden, my favorite hiking partner in New York state, and to
Lori Greene, my favorite hiking partner out West*

Book Design: Nelson Sa
Contributing Editor: Jennifer Ceaser
Photo Credits: Cover, p. 5, 6 © Index Stock Photography Inc.; p. 9 © Kevin
R. Morris/Corbis; p. 11 © Index Stock Photography Inc.; p. 13 © Phil
Schermeister/Corbis; p. 14 © Earl & Nazima Kowall/Corbis; p. 19 ©
Raymond Gehman/Corbis; p. 20 © Joel W. Rogers/Corbis; p. 23 © Phil
Schermeister/Corbis; p. 24 © Phil Schermeister/Corbis; p. 27 © Dave G.
Houser/Corbis; p. 29 © David Muench/Corbis; p. 31 © Index Stock
Photography Inc.; p. 32, 34 © Phil Schermeister/Corbis; p. 37 © Roy
Corral/Corbis; p. 38 © Phil Schermeister/Corbis; p. 41 © Index Stock
Photography Inc.

Library of Congress Cataloging-in-Publication Data

Hooks, Kristine.
    Essential hiking for teens / by Kristine Hooks.
        p. cm. – (Outdoor life)
    Includes bibliographical references and index.
    Summary: Provides information on conditioning for hiking, first aid and
survival skills, what to wear, safety tips, and more.
    ISBN 0-516-23357-2 (lib. bdg.) – ISBN 0-516-23557-5 (pbk.)
    1. Hiking for children—Juvenile literature. [1. Hiking.] I. Title. II Outdoor
life (Children's Press)

GV199.54.H66 2000
796.51—dc21

                                                    00-025427

CONTENTS

Introduction

When most people think of hiking, they think it involves walking uphill, such as up a mountain. However, people also hike across flat areas, such as meadows and forests. Basically, any walking that you do to experience your surroundings on foot could be considered hiking. Even a trek through the city is a type of hike!

A hike can be for as short as an hour or as long as several days. Hikes that can be done in one to eight hours are called day hikes. Longer hiking trips involve walking for several hours per day, over two or more days. It's important to be in shape and have the right equipment when you go on these hikes. This book will provide you with the essential information to become a skilled, safe hiker.

Hiking uphill in the mountains is one type of hike.

1
Before You Hike

It's important to be in good physical shape before you go hiking.

Before you hit your first trail, you should spend some time preparing in two important areas. Physical fitness and first aid/survival skills are very important. A little prehiking study in these areas should make your hike a safe and enjoyable experience.

SHAPE UP

Before you start any new physical activity, you should take a look at your current physical condition. You need to know the level of physical exercise you can do and for how long you can do it. Ask yourself these questions:

- Do you do some kind of cardiovascular exercise for at least thirty minutes a day, three times a week? (Playing basketball, running, walking, swimming, etc.)
- Can you walk, steadily and quickly, for at least one hour?
- Can you run at least 1 mile (1.5 km)?

• Can you walk up several flights of stairs without stopping?

If you can answer yes to two or more of the questions, you are most likely up to the challenge of hiking. However, you may find that hiking uses muscles that you did not even know you had.

If you answered no to three or more of the questions, then you should take at least a few weeks to build up your endurance. Begin by taking walks at a fast pace. Walk as far as you can without becoming exhausted. Do this every day if you can, slowly increasing the distance of your walks. In addition, add regular stair climbing to your daily activities. Take the stairs instead of the elevator or escalator when possible. Go up and down several flights of

Hiking uses muscles you may never know you had.

stairs for five to fifteen minutes at a time until you can do so without feeling out of breath.

You also should work on strengthening your abdominal (stomach) muscles as part of your overall exercise program. Lay on your back, with your legs bent and your knees up. With your hands behind your head, use your stomach muscles to lift your upper body off the floor, until your shoulders are curled in toward your knees. Strong abdominal muscles will make your posture better and your back stronger. You will find hiking is much easier if you have strong abdominal muscles.

If you are not sure about your fitness level, check with a doctor first and start out doing easy hikes.

FIRST AID/SURVIVAL SKILLS

You should know basic first aid skills and outdoor survival techniques before you head off on your first hike. Even if you are going with experienced hikers, make sure you know what to do, too. What happens if the first aid expert of the group is the one who gets injured? You can save the day if you know the information to help an injured friend.

Also, anyone who takes off into the wilderness, whether on a day hike or a longer hiking trip, should know what to do in case he or she gets lost. You can find first aid and outdoor survival guides at your local library, in a bookstore, or at a sporting goods store.

Look for a guide that has pictures and text that you can easily understand. Make sure that the book you select fits comfortably in your backpack so that you can carry it on your hike. Use your first aid and outdoor survival guide to become familiar with all of the items in your first aid kit (see page 40). Read your guide to learn how to make a fire in an emergency and how to build a temporary shelter.

You should know how to perform basic first aid skills, such as bandaging a wound, before you go on a hike.

You also will need to know how to use a compass. A compass is an essential item for any hiking trip, but it will not do you any good if you do not know how to use it.

TAKE A CLASS

You may want to take a first aid course and an orienteering class. Orienteering will help you to know where you are at all times. An orienteering class will teach you how to use a compass and how to read a topographical (land) map. These courses usually are offered through your local public high school, community center, or community college.

You can join an organization, such as the Boy Scouts or Girl Scouts, to learn more about hiking. Another good way to get familiar with hiking is to join a local hiking club or national hiking association, such as the National Campers and Hikers Association and the American Hiking Society.

You need to know how to use a compass so that you know where you are at all times.

2
Hiking: Gear and Supplies

Hiking gear should include boots, appropriate clothing, and a backpack.

The three most basic things you will need for hiking are (1) sturdy walking shoes or boots, (2) weather-appropriate, layered clothing, and (3) a lightweight backpack.

FOOTWEAR

Trail hiking, especially through rocky, hilly areas, requires special footwear. Your basic gym shoes or street shoes will not provide enough stability or protection. One choice is cross-trainer shoes with thick soles and a slightly higher top than your average running shoe. Another choice is a lightweight boot.

All footwear should have good traction (to keep from slipping). The uppers should be made mostly from fabric. Fabric uppers make the shoe more lightweight (you do not want to carry extra pounds up hills) and breathable (to keep your feet drier).

There are times, however, when you may need leather boots. Wear them if you are going to be carrying a heavy load over long distances or hiking through a very rugged area.

If you buy new shoes or boots for hiking, break them in before starting up the trail. Wear them for walks around your neighborhood and around the house. If you notice any areas that seem irritated, plan ahead by wearing bandages or extra socks to avoid blisters.

CLOTHING

You want to stay warm and dry when the weather is cold, and cool and dry when it's hot. Dressing in light, loose layers is best for both conditions.

In cold weather:
- Start with a long-sleeve shirt made of polyester, silk, or a synthetic (man-made) fabric, such as polypropylene. These fabrics allow moisture (such as sweat) to evaporate.

- Next, layer on two or three loose shirts. These loose layers keep you dry, while air pockets trapped between the layers help to keep you warm.
- Your outer layer should be loose-fitting and waterproof. Don't bundle so tightly inside your jacket that air cannot circulate (get in and out).
- As for pants, use a similar system of layering. For example, silk long johns can be worn under sweatpants. Avoid wearing jeans because they take a very long time to dry if they get wet.
- Do not wear all-cotton clothing next to your skin. If you get wet (from rain or sweating), the cotton will trap moisture. Then it will be difficult for your skin to dry off and warm up.
- You should always be prepared for rainy conditions in any season. Bring along a nylon windbreaker or a rain poncho.

In warm weather:
- Layer a light-colored T-shirt with a light-weight, light-colored, long-sleeve shirt. These layers will protect you from sunburn.
- Long, lightweight, breathable pants offer good protection from the sun's rays. Consider buying lightweight hiking pants with legs that unzip so that you can wear them either as pants or shorts.

No matter what the weather, always bring appropriate headgear. A lightweight hat with a large brim will protect your face from sunburn. Remember that temperatures can drop at any time, especially if you are high up in the mountains. Always carry a winter hat or make sure that your jacket has a hood. Cover your head when it starts to get cold, to keep in body heat.

Loss of body heat can lead to a dangerous condition called hypothermia. Hypothermia happens when your body is exposed to wind, wetness, and cold temperatures. A person's body begins to lose heat faster than the heat can be replaced. The temperature of the body begins to drop. A person begins to shiver, lose concentration, and breathe more slowly. He or she must be taken to a warm place as soon as possible.

Always cover your head during cold or wet weather to avoid hypothermia.

BACKPACK

Unless you are going on overnight trips, you can use just about any type of backpack to hike. You can probably use your school backpack. Just be sure that it has sturdy straps and that it is lightweight. The backpack also should have enough room to hold food, water, and other essentials.

SUPPLIES

What will you put in your backpack? You'll need drinking water and food for the road.

Proper hydration (the balance of water in your body) is very important when hiking. A good rule of thumb is to bring between 64 and 96 ounces (2 to 3 liters) of water, per person, for a full day of hiking. Don't count on finding drinkable water sources on the trail. You will not find water fountains in the woods, and you cannot be sure that natural water sources are safe to drink from.

Drink a lot of water for several days before your hike to help prevent dehydration. Drink at least eight glasses of water each day and avoid eating food that has a lot of salt.

Hikers need to bring energy-rich foods that pack plenty of carbohydrates (sugar and starches), fat, and protein. Your diet should include a mix of fruits and grains that will travel well and that are low in salt. Oranges, bananas, apples, and pears are good choices.

Fill plastic baggies with whole-grain cereal, individual cereal bars, or granola bars for a healthy snack. Unsalted nuts mixed with raisins or other dried fruits will give your body protein. Be sure to eat regularly to keep up your energy level.

Food and water aren't the only essential items you should bring on a hike. Be sure that the following supplies are in your backpack:

- map of your hiking area
- compass
- whistle (in case you need to call for help)
- flashlight (with extra batteries)
- multitooled instrument, such as a Swiss army knife
- small pack of tissues or a roll of toilet paper
- waterproof matches (in a resealable plastic bag)
- first aid kit
- first aid/wilderness survival guide book
- plastic bags for carrying out trash

- sunscreen and sunglasses
- insect repellent
- warm clothing and rain gear
- water-purifying tablets

You also may want to bring binoculars to spot interesting wildlife. A camera, pen, and paper can help you to record your journey in pictures and words.

One essential item to bring along is a map of your hiking area.

3
Making the Most of Your Trail Time

Use a trail map to choose your hiking route.

Technically, you could just walk out the door to your house or apartment and start "hiking." However, when people talk about hiking, they usually mean walking along a marked trail. Hiking trails can be found in parks, forests, and protected wildlife conservation areas.

FIND YOUR ROUTE

Check your local library for guides to marked hiking trails in and around your area. A camping or sporting goods store should have a good selection of local hiking guides and trail maps. These maps and guides will give information about how to get to a trail, either by car or by public transportation.

Another resource is your state or local parks department, which are listed in your telephone book. These offices will give you information about hiking opportunities in your area. (For

Hiking Tip

Start a notebook with information about trails you have hiked. Also keep information about trails or hiking locations that you have read about and would like to try. This way, you will always have an idea for a place to hike.

information about national parks in your area, check out the National Parks System Web site at *www.nps.gov.*)

CHOOSE YOUR TRAIL

Your guide or map should contain important information about the level of difficulty of the hiking trail. It also should include the approximate amount of time required to complete the hike. Trail guides and maps should tell you whether the trail is easy, moderate, strenuous (hard), or very strenuous.

Easy hikes are good for new and casual hikers. These hikes take place on terrain (land) that is mostly flat or only slightly hilly. Moderate trails are good for the intermediate hiker. They are of average distance and have slightly difficult terrain. Strenuous and very strenuous hikes are longer and more difficult than easy or moderate hikes. They take place over steep and rocky terrain, which can make a hike very challenging.

This trail sign indicates the names of trails and their lengths (in miles).

MAKE A PLAN

The starting point of any trail is the trailhead. When you arrive at the trailhead, make sure that you have enough daylight hours to complete your hike. Also, keep in mind where and when you will be finishing up the hike so that people know your hiking plans.

The Mighty Appalachian

The Appalachian Trail was the first trail to be named a National Scenic Trail by the United States Congress. It is approximately 2,100 miles (3,400 km) long. The trail runs along the top of the Appalachian Mountains, which stretch from Maine to Georgia. Hiking every mile of the entire Appalachian Trail takes between five and six months. Every year, about 1,500 people start out on the journey but only about 300 people finish it. For the average hiker, the Appalachian Trail offers opportunities for day hikes and short hiking trips.

Part of the Appalachian Trail runs through the Great Smoky Mountains of Tennessee.

Hiking Tip

You can make any trail an in-and-out hike. Follow the trail for about one-half of the time you want to be hiking. Then turn around and follow the trail back to your starting point. If most of your trail is uphill, keep in mind that the return trip (going mostly downhill) will go faster.

TYPES OF TRAILS

Where you end your hike will depend on the type of trail that you are hiking. Trail types include a loop trail, an in-and-out trail, or a point-to-point trail. Loop trails and in-and-out trails both start and end at the same point. A loop trail takes you along a circular path. An in-and-out trail leads you to a certain point and then back along the same straight path. If you're hiking a point-to-point trail, you will need to plan ahead. With a point-to-point trail, you start at one point and end at another. This means that, at the end of the hike, you will need transportation back to where you started.

Be sure that you know the type of trail that you will be hiking before you start.

TRAIL TIMES

To estimate the time of your hike, allow one hour for every 3 miles (4.8 km) of flat terrain that you'll be hiking. Add thirty minutes for every 1,000 feet (303 m) that the altitude (height) increases. The altitude should be listed in your guide or on signs along the trail. Keep in mind that the higher up you are, the thinner the air is. Thin air is harder to breathe, because it has less oxygen. If your body is not getting enough oxygen, it has to work harder to get your muscles to work. At higher altitudes, expect to go slower. Take more breaks and travel more slowly.

TREAD CAREFULLY AND SAFELY

Here are some tips to make you a better and safer hiker:

- Warm up before you begin hiking. Do some simple stretches, focusing on the muscles

The higher the altitude, the more breaks you will need to take.

in your legs. Then run in place for a few minutes.

- If you are traveling with a group, agree to set a pace that is comfortable for everyone. The people who are moving most quickly will stop hiking at a particular time, then wait for the others in the group to catch up.
- No matter how quickly or slowly you are traveling, stop for water breaks regularly. Take at least a ten-minute break for every fifty minutes of hiking. Take short, frequent breaks to catch your breath when going up a hill.
- Look at your trail map regularly. You will improve your map-reading skills and can get back on track if you accidentally get off the trail. Also, most trails are marked with colored markers. Follow these markers to be sure that you are staying on the path.
- Pay attention to where you are stepping at all times. When you run across areas that

It's important to take breaks and drink plenty of water when you hike.

are wet or damp, test out your shoes' traction before moving on.

- Be careful crossing any body of water, such as a stream or small river. (You usually will not cross water on marked hiking trails.) Use a strong walking stick to test each step before you take it, checking for changes in the depth of the water. Do not cross in spots where the current is running fast.

- Be aware of your surroundings. Remember that the woods are home to other animals, including snakes and bears. If you see a snake, walk around it in a wide path. If you see a bear, slowly back away from the bear, with your arms waving in the air above your head, talking in a loud, calm voice.

- If you get lost or separated from the rest of your group, do not panic. Stay where you are and blow your whistle to let others know where you are. Don't start moving or you will be harder to find.

You must step very carefully if you are crossing any body of water.

THE BENEFITS OF HIKING

Hiking is both a challenging and a rewarding experience. Hiking can be tiring, but it is also great exercise. You will find that hiking gives you an opportunity to experience nature and the world around you. Hiking also gives you the chance to spend quiet, peaceful times with close friends or family.

Hiking with your family can be very rewarding.

Leave No Trace

Following these rules will help reduce the wear-and-tear on the environment. Doing your part will keep the outdoors beautiful for future generations.

- **Stay on marked trails.** Don't trample plants or wildflowers.
- **Dispose of garbage properly.** Pack out what you pack in! Bring extra garbage bags with you to bag up trash and carry it out of the park.
- **Leave what you find.** Leave the trail in the same condition in which you found it. Of course, if you find someone else's trash along the trail, pick it up and take it back out with you.
- **Respect wildlife.** For your own safety and the safety of the animals, keep your distance from them. Animals live in the woods, so don't do anything that will destroy their habitat. Don't pollute rivers, streams, and lakes with soap or human waste. Don't harm the plants and trees, which they need for food and to build their homes. Don't feed animals human food. Keep your noise level down so you don't scare or disturb wildlife.
- **Be considerate.** Don't talk so loudly that you bother other hikers. Always be helpful and courteous to other people on the trails.

SAFETY TIPS

Always pack a first aid kit with Band-Aids and bandages, hydrogen peroxide, antibiotic creams, and some common painkillers (aspirin, Tylenol, and Advil). Add some tweezers for removing splinters and pulling off ticks. Bug spray is also a good idea. Always carry a first aid guide, too.

Avoiding Common Health Problems

- Dehydration can be avoided by drinking sufficient amounts of water and other fluids throughout the day. Drink more if you are sweating a lot.
- Sunburn can occur in the winter as well as in the summer. Apply a high SPF sunblock and wear a wide-brimmed hat.
- Sprained ankles can be avoided by wearing good fitting shoes with strong ankle support.
- If serious injuries occur, send one person in your hiking party for help. Have one person stay behind with the injured person.

Remember these very important hiking tips:

- Be in shape before you begin your hike.
- Always allow yourself enough daylight to finish your hike.
- Always dress sensibly and for any kind of weather.
- Learn how to read maps and a compass.
- Act in a mature and safe manner at all times. Be aware of your environment.

Always carry a first aid kit. It should look much like the one below.

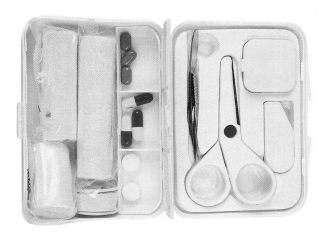

NEW WORDS

abdominal related to the stomach

altitude the distance or height that a point on land is above sea level

cardiovascular dealing with the heart and blood vessels; cardiovascular exercise is any exercise that increases the heart rate to your target rate, for improved heart health

circulation flow or movement, like the flow of blood through blood vessels or the flow of air through a space or area

compass a device for determining direction (north, south, east, or west)

dehydration loss of water and bodily fluids

hydration balance of water in your body

hypothermia a dangerous condition in which one's body temperature is well below normal

in-and-out trail a trail that leads you to a certain point and then back along the same straight path

loop trail a trail that follows a circular path

orienteering to know where a position is using a compass and map

point-to-point trail a trail that starts at one point and ends at another

poncho loose rain clothing that is often made of plastic

strenuous difficult

synthetic man-made

terrain the features of the land, such as hills

topographical map map which shows various distances and heights of an area, with details showing rivers, lakes, and mountains

traction something that prevents you from slipping

trailhead the start of a trail

RESOURCES

American Hiking Society
www.americanhiking.org
This organization offers state-by-state information about hiking clubs, volunteer opportunities, and trail conservation efforts.

Appalachian Trail Conference
www.atconf.org
This site has everything you need to know about the Appalachian Trail. It includes maps, frequently asked questions about the Trail, permit and regulation information, and volunteer opportunities.

National Park Foundation
www.nationalparks.org/guide/national-trails.htm
Click on a region of the United States to find out where the national parks are in your state. Then find out more about the national scenic and historic trails in your area.

North American Trails
www.natrails.com
This organization offers multiday trail hiking trips for teens all across the country. The site includes a photo gallery, chat room, and links to other hiking sites.

the backpacker.com
www.thebackpacker.com
The "beginner's corner"on this site contains information about what to bring on hiking trips and how to behave on a trail. A database lets you find out about trails in your area. There are directions on how to get to trails, maps, and hikers' comments about trails.

The Sierra Club
www.sierraclub.org/chapters
Search for your local Sierra Club chapter and learn about organized group hikes and nature conservation efforts.

FOR FURTHER READING

Books

Andryszewski, Tricia. *Step by Step Along the Appalachian Trail*. New York: Twenty-First Century Books, Inc., 1998.

Berger, Karen. *Hiking and Backpacking: A Complete Guide*. New York: W.W. Norton & Co., 1995.

Boy Scouts of America Staff. *Hiking*. Irving, TX: Boy Scouts of America, 1996.

Foster, Lynne. *Take A Hike! The Sierra Club Kid's Guide to Hiking and Backpacking*. New York: Little, Brown & Co., 1991.

McManners, Hugh. *101 Essential Tips—Hiking*. New York: DK Publishing, 1998.

McManners, Hugh. *The Backpacker's Handbook*. New York: DK Publishing, 1995.

Wood, Robert S. *Dayhiker—Walking for Fitness, Fun & Adventure*. Berkeley, CA: Ten Speed Press, 1991.

Werner, Doug. *Backpacker's Start-Up: A Beginner's Guide to Hiking and Backpacking*. Chula Vista, CA: Tracks Publishing, 1999.

Magazines

Hooked on the Outdoors Magazine
P.O. Box 888637
Dunwoody, GA 30356-9916
Web site: *www.hookedontheoutdoors.com*

Outdoor Explorer
2 Park Avenue
10th Floor
New York, NY 10013
Web site: *www.outdoorexplorer.com*

Index

ABOUT THE AUTHOR

Kristine Hooks is a lawyer living in New York City. She developed a love of hiking while attending summer camp in the Blue Ridge Mountains.